WILDLIFE WORLDS

EUROPE

TIM HARRIS

CRABTREE
PUBLISHING COMPANY
WWW.CRABTREEBOOKS.COM

CRABTREE
PUBLISHING COMPANY
WWW.CRABTREEBOOKS.COM

Published in Canada
Crabtree Publishing
616 Welland Avenue
St. Catharines, ON
L2M 5V6

Published in the United States
Crabtree Publishing
PMB 59051
350 Fifth Ave, 59th Floor
New York, NY 10118

Published in 2020 by Crabtree Publishing Company

First published in Great Britain in 2019 by The Watts Publishing Group
Copyright © The Watts Publishing Group 2019

Printed in the U.S.A./122019/CG20191101

With thanks to the Nature Picture Library

Author: Tim Harris

Editorial director: Kathy Middleton

Editors: Amy Pimperton, Robin Johnson

Series Designer: Nic Davies smartdesignstudio.co.uk

Photo researchers: Rachelle Morris (Nature Picture Library), Laura Sutherland (Nature Picture Library), Diana Morris

Proofreader: Wendy Scavuzzo

Production coordinator and prepress: Tammy McGarr

Print coordinator: Katherine Berti

Every attempt has been made to clear copyright.
Should there be any inadvertent omission,
please apply to the publisher for rectification.

Photo credits:
Alamy: Amanda Pharyos 15tl.
Nature PL: Ingo Amdt 15tr; Barry Bland 29br; Juan Manuel Borrero 22br; Peter Cairns 2b, 28c; Stephen Dalton 9br, 19b; Martin Gabriel 3c, 17bc; Angelo Gandolfi 22–23t; Patricio Robles Gil front cover b; Erland Haarland 21t; Klein & Hubert 17bl; Pete Oxford 21bl; Michel Poinsignan 7tr; Jean E Roche 18–19c; The Big Picture 24; Nick Upton 12bl; Markus Varesvuo: 17c; Wild Wonders of Europe/Orsolya Haarberg 27br/Giesbers 17br/Lilja 6b/ Lundgren 9bl/ Smit 8–9t/Varesvuo 15b/Zupanc 16; Sven Zacek 11tr.
Shutterstock: Belizar 3t, 8bl; Biggunsband 12–13c; Bildagenteur Zoonar GmbH 3b, 19tr; Aleksander Bolbot back cover tl, 2t, 10–11c; Mike Caunt front cover t, 25tc; Chuckstop 5c; Daniel Dunca back cover tr, 23br; Frank Fichtmueller 23tr; Giedrilus 4b, 25c, 32t; Paulis Giovanni 7tl; liluta goean 9cr; Andrey Gudkov 19tl, 30t; J. Helgason 26–27c, 31t; Jaro68 17tl; Lukas Juocas 29cl; Szczepan Klejbuk 1, 11b; Piotr Krzeslak 21br; Liane M 20c, 20bl; Pablo Manzi 5t; Mark Medcalf 4t; Marek Mierzejewski 25tl; Ondrej Prosicky 27bl; Ben Queenborough 25tr; Stella Photography back cover tcr, 14bl, 30b; Andrew Sutton 29t; Marek R Swadzba back cover tcl, 5b, 10bl, 13cr; Taviphoto 13b; Wead 14t; k west 6–7c; Shaun Wilkinson 13tr; Vladimir Wrangel 26bl, 32b.

Library and Archives Canada Cataloguing in Publication

Title: Europe / Tim Harris.
Names: Harris, Tim (Ornithologist), author.
Description: Series statement: Wildlife worlds |
   Previously published: London: Franklin Watts, 2019. | Includes index.
Identifiers: Canadiana (print) 20190200650 |
   Canadiana (ebook) 20190200669 |
   ISBN 9780778776802 (hardcover) |
   ISBN 9780778776864 (softcover) |
   ISBN 9781427125347 (HTML)
Subjects: LCSH: Animals—Europe—Juvenile literature. | LCSH: Habitat (Ecology)—Europe—Juvenile literature. | LCSH: Natural history—Europe—Juvenile literature. | LCSH: Europe—Juvenile literature.
Classification: LCC QL253 .H37 2020 | DDC j591.94—dc23

Library of Congress Cataloging-in-Publication Data

Names: Harris, Tim (Ornithologist), author.
Title: Europe / Tim Harris.
Description: New York : Crabtree Publishing Company, 2020. |
   Series: Wildlife worlds | Includes index.
Identifiers: LCCN 2019043613 (print) | LCCN 2019043614 (ebook) |
   ISBN 9780778776802 (hardcover) |
   ISBN 9780778776864 (paperback) |
   ISBN 9781427125347 (ebook)
Subjects: LCSH: Animals--Europe--Juvenile literature. | Plants--Europe--Juvenile literature.
Classification: LCC QL253 .H37 2020 (print) | LCC QL253 (ebook) |
   DDC 591.94--dc23
LC record available at https://lccn.loc.gov/2019043613
LC ebook record available at https://lccn.loc.gov/2019043614

Contents

European Continent

The European continent is surrounded by the Arctic and Atlantic oceans to the north and west, and the Mediterranean and Black seas to the south. In the east, it is separated from Asia by the Ural and Caucasus mountains.

Europe's climate varies greatly. In the far north, temperatures remain below freezing throughout the winter months. The great plains of Russia and Eastern Europe are freezing cold in winter, but baking hot in summer. Southern Europe has a pleasant climate: hot and dry in summer and warm for the rest of the year. About one-third of Europe is covered by forest. There are also large areas of natural grassland.

ATLANTIC PUFFIN

Europe has several high mountain ranges, including the Alps and the Pyrenees.

RED DEER

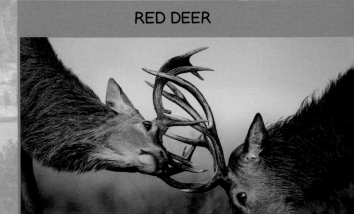

4

The continent's two longest rivers are the Danube and the Volga.

Arctic Ocean

Iceland

Lofoten Islands

Arctic Circle

Europe's largest **glaciers** are on the island of Iceland.

To the Ural Mountains and the border of Asia →

Caledonian Forest

North Sea

Atlantic Ocean

Baltic Sea

Volga River

Black Forest

Bialowieza Forest

Danube Delta

Caspian Sea

Picos de Europa

Rhône River

Alps

Danube River

Caucasus

Pyrenees

Camargue

Black Sea

Plitvice Lakes

Extremadura

Aegean Sea

Russia, the largest country in the world, lies in Europe and Asia.

Mount Etna

Santorini

Mediterranean Sea

At 15,774 feet (4,808 m), Mont Blanc is the highest mountain in the Alps.

LONGHORN BEETLE

Santorini

The stunning island of Santorini rises out of the Aegean Sea southeast of mainland Greece. Santorini, which is officially called Thira, and other islands surround a large, oval **lagoon**.

The islands are all that remain of a volcano that erupted violently about 3,600 years ago. Gigantic cliffs of volcanic rock rise out of the ocean. Villages of white houses are built into the steep slopes. The islands have no rivers or lakes because rainwater runs straight into the **porous** rocks.

The lagoon formed when seawater filled the volcano's **caldera**. It measures about 7.5 miles (12 km) across and 1,312 feet (400 m) deep.

Many old olive trees grow on Santorini and nearby islands. People eat their fruit and use it to make olive oil.

Eleonora's falcons build their nests on cliffs in Santorini. They leave their nests to hunt dragonflies and small birds.

Insects on Santorini include praying mantises. Praying mantises, like this European mantis, are large insects that grab **prey** with their front legs.

Danube River

The Danube is Europe's second-longest river. It starts in Germany's Black Forest and widens as it winds 1,770 miles (2,850 km) through 10 countries on its way to the Black Sea. Many of Europe's great cities were built along this river.

The Danube is rich in fish, otters, and other aquatic animals. When it gets close to the Black Sea, the river divides into several channels and flows slowly between vast **reedbeds**. This area is the Danube **Delta**. It is home to most of the world's white pelicans and many thousands of other birds.

Otters are playful animals that swim fast underwater to catch fish.

The Danube sturgeon is a very rare fish. It can grow more than 7 feet (2 m) long and swims from the Black Sea up the river to lay its eggs.

The Danube flows through forests, farmland, and **marshes** on its way to the Black Sea.

GREAT WHITE PELICAN

A male emperor dragonfly will defend its **territory** from other dragonflies.

Bialowieza Forest

A huge, ancient forest once covered most of Eastern Europe. Although most of it has been cut down for farmland, a large area in Belarus and Poland called the Bialowieza Forest remains.

Bialowieza is a **dense** forest of spruce, pine, alder, oak, and birch trees. Many are very old. One tree, the Patriarch Oak, is more than 550 years old! All of the world's wild European bison live in the forest, which is also home to woodpeckers, storks, and other birds. Many beautiful flowers grow in Bialowieza's wet meadows.

Many butterflies live in and around the forest, including the stunning Camberwell beauty.

When trees fall in the dense forest, they create openings in the **canopy** above. This allows sunshine to reach the forest floor and helps young trees to grow. Dead trees provide nest holes for woodpeckers, as well as homes for insects and many other **invertebrates**.

Black woodpeckers use their beaks to drill holes in trees so they can feed on invertebrates living inside.

The European bison is Europe's largest **native** land animal.

Plitvice Lakes National Park

In the Velebit Mountains of Croatia, the Korana River tumbles down **rapids** and waterfalls. It passes through a chain of 16 lakes called the Plitvice Lakes. Each lake is lower than the previous one. This is one of the most beautiful places in Europe.

Trout and other fish swim in the Plitvice Lakes. Surrounding the crystal-clear waters of the lakes are woods and meadows. Bears, wolves, and wildcats such as lynx live in the forest. Colorful orchids and other wildflowers grow in the meadows, while bats make their homes in the many caves in the **limestone** rocks.

Veliki Slap is the highest waterfall at Plitvice. Water plunges 256 feet (78 m) over a limestone cliff and splashes into the lake below.

Lynx are fearsome **predators**. They hunt on the ground but can also climb trees and even swim to catch fish.

Many kinds of insects live at Plitvice, including dragonflies, butterflies, and longhorn beetles (below).

The horned viper is the most **venomous** snake in Croatia.

Mount Etna

Mount Etna, on the Italian island of Sicily, is one of the biggest and most active volcanoes in the world. Every few years, spectacular **eruptions** burst from one of the four **craters** at its **summit**.

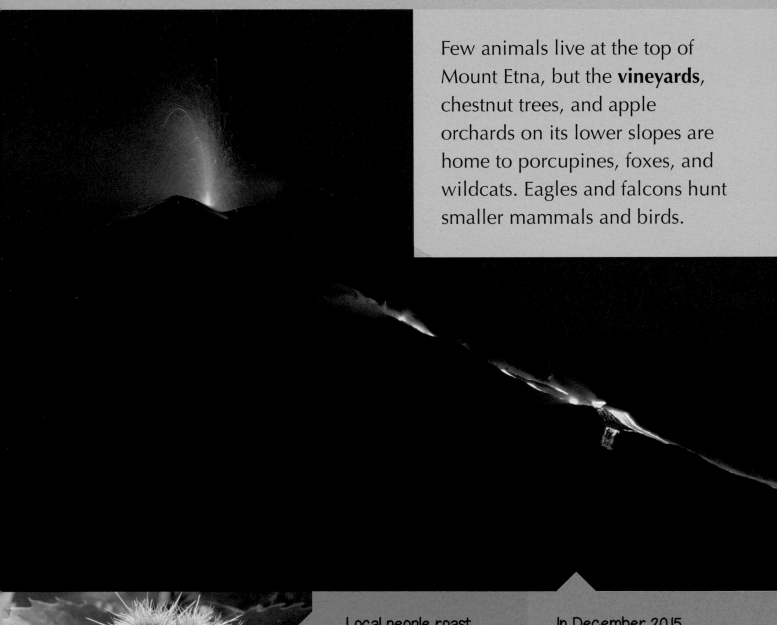

Few animals live at the top of Mount Etna, but the **vineyards**, chestnut trees, and apple orchards on its lower slopes are home to porcupines, foxes, and wildcats. Eagles and falcons hunt smaller mammals and birds.

Local people roast chestnuts from sweet chestnut trees, some of which are hundreds of years old.

In December 2015, Mount Etna erupted at night. It lit up the sky and sent a cloud of ash 2 miles (3 km) into the air.

If threatened, a crested porcupine charges backward into its attacker to stab it with sharp spines called quills.

The Mediterranean black widow spider has a deadly bite.

A bee-eaters' favorite foods are bees and wasps. Before eating its prey, the multicolored bird bashes the bee or wasp on a hard surface to kill it and remove the stinger.

Alps

The Alps stretch across eight countries and form Europe's highest mountain range. Hundreds of peaks rise more than 9,840 feet (3,000 m) above sea level. Glaciers have carved them into jagged shapes, with knife-like ridges and pointed summits.

Broad-leaved trees, such as oak, beech, and ash, grow on the lower slopes of the Alps. They are replaced by pine trees and dwarf shrubs at higher **altitudes**. Above the **tree line**, **alpine** meadows are covered with snow for most of the year but filled with colorful flowers in summer. Mountain goats, bears, and large squirrels called marmots are some of the animals that live in the mountains.

16

The Matterhorn is one of the highest mountains in the Alps, towering 14,692 feet (4,478 m) above the landscape. Its sides are so steep that no one was able to climb to its summit until 1865.

A golden eagle uses its strong talons to pick up rabbits and marmots from the ground, then kills the prey with its hooked beak.

Alpine marmots **hibernate** during the winter months.

Fire salamanders live in the **foothills** of the Alps. They spend much of their time hidden under logs or rocks.

The small flowers of edelweiss bloom when the mountain snow melts between July and September.

Camargue

Where the mighty Rhône River meets the Mediterranean Sea on the south coast of France lies the Camargue region—Europe's largest delta. This vast marshy plain has many lakes and pools surrounded by reedbeds.

Flamingos, herons, and other long-legged birds wade in the shallow waters of the Camargue in search of food. Birds of prey such as eagles and harriers hunt overhead, and thousands of warblers and other small birds build their nests in the reeds. Camargue horses and cattle graze on the grasslands between the lakes.

Thousands of small birds, mammals, and amphibians make their homes in the Camargue's reedbeds.

Herds of Camargue horses run wild through the marshes.

Penduline tits are tiny birds who build nests that hang from tree branches. The nests are made from animal hair, spiderwebs, and pieces of leaves.

Male Mediterranean tree frogs croak loudly in spring to attract mates. The noise of many frogs croaking at once can be deafening!

Extremadura

In winter, the rolling grasslands of the Extremadura region of Spain are wet, **barren**, and cold. In spring, the area warms up and comes alive with the blooms of millions of wildflowers. By midsummer, the region becomes baking hot and dry.

While some areas are treeless, other places have a mix of open woodland and grass, called dehesa. Here, thousands of long-necked, long-legged birds called cranes feed on fallen acorns during the winter. In spring, these birds fly away to breeding grounds. They are replaced by colorful birds, such as bee-eaters and rollers, that have **migrated** from Africa.

Cattle graze among the trees of the dehesa landscape.

Rollers often perch high on posts, trees, or overhead wires. From there, they watch for small snakes, mice, or frogs to swoop down on to eat.

The beautifully patterned false smooth snake has enough **venom** to kill a lizard, but not enough to harm humans.

Many cranes spend the winter in the Extremadura region of Spain. Then they fly much farther north to breed in Denmark, Norway, and Sweden.

Picos de Europa

A mountain range rises dramatically near the northern coast of Spain. Called the Picos de Europa, this range has been shaped by slow-moving glaciers and the action of flowing water.

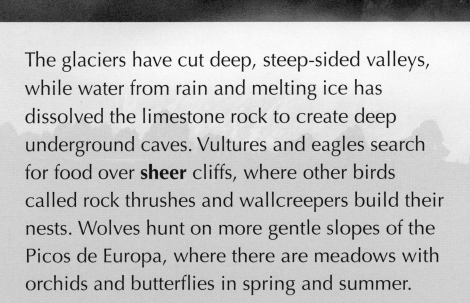

NARANJO DE BULNES

The glaciers have cut deep, steep-sided valleys, while water from rain and melting ice has dissolved the limestone rock to create deep underground caves. Vultures and eagles search for food over **sheer** cliffs, where other birds called rock thrushes and wallcreepers build their nests. Wolves hunt on more gentle slopes of the Picos de Europa, where there are meadows with orchids and butterflies in spring and summer.

The bright-yellow flowers of Pyrenean lilies can be seen from May to July, but only at high altitudes.

The sides of Naranjo de Bulnes are almost straight up, so they are a challenge for any rock climber. The summit of the mountain is more than 8,200 feet (2,500 m) high.

Sure-footed chamois are adapted to climbing the very steep slopes.

More than 150 different kinds of butterflies live in the Picos de Europa, including the spectacular swallowtail.

Colorful wallcreepers are at home on bare rock faces.

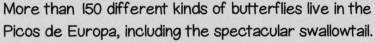

Caledonian Forest

The Caledonian Forest has grown in the highlands of Scotland for about 9,000 years. Although much of this pine forest has been cut down, some large areas remain.

The Caledonian Forest is home to red deer, pine martens, red squirrels, and a few species of wildcats. Birds of prey called ospreys plunge feetfirst into the slow-moving waters of the River Spey to catch salmon and other fish. Crossbills feed on pinecones, while larger birds called capercaillies eat evergreen needles during the winter, when snow carpets the ground.

Pine forest covers the lower slopes of the Cairngorm Mountains. The tops of the mountains are treeless and often hidden in clouds. Freshwater lakes, called lochs, in the forest are home to swans, ducks, and other waterbirds.

Named for their color, strawberry spiders live in damp clearings in the forest.

Atlantic salmon swim from the ocean to **spawn** upstream in rivers, such as the Spey.

Crested tits spend their whole lives in the Caledonian Forest.

Each autumn, male red deer fight each other for power. These battles, called ruts, can be very violent.

Iceland

In the far north of the Atlantic Ocean, the island country of Iceland sits just below the Arctic Circle. Icy glaciers cover much of its surface, and it also has many active and **dormant** volcanoes.

Rivers carrying **meltwater** from glaciers plunge over spectacular waterfalls on their way to the ocean. There are hundreds of geysers, or fountains of boiling water, that regularly spurt from the ground. Although Iceland is cold and windy for much of the year, it is mild enough in the summer to support many birds and flowering plants. There are no native reptiles or amphibians on the island.

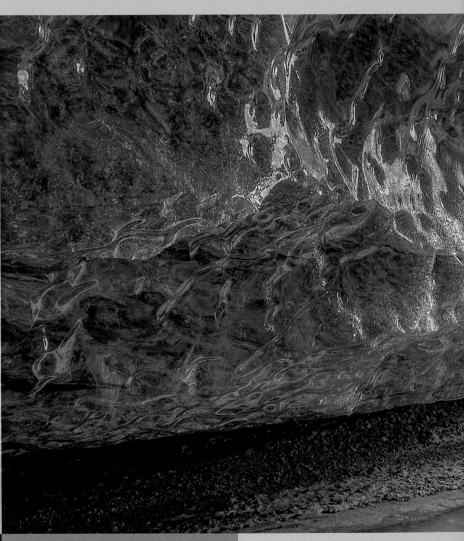

Sea urchins live on the seabed in coastal waters around Iceland. They feed on barnacles and **marine** worms.

The Arctic fox, which has snow-white fur in winter, is Iceland's only native land mammal.

Ice caves form during the summer when water carves out areas beneath glaciers such as Vatnajökull, the largest glacier in Europe. In winter, it is too cold for water to flow, so these areas become empty caves.

Harlequin ducks spend the winter at the coast. In spring, they return to fast-flowing rivers to raise their young.

Lofoten Islands

The Lofoten Islands rise spectacularly from the ocean off the coast of northern Norway. Sheer cliffs tower above the sea, with thousands of seabirds nesting on their ledges. Narrow **inlets**, such as Trollfjord, were carved there by ancient glaciers.

The snow-dusted cliffs of Festhelltinden Mountain loom over red cabins used by fishers.

The Lofoten Islands are made up of six major islands and hundreds of smaller ones. Despite being north of the Arctic Circle, temperatures rise above freezing even during the winter because of the warming effect of the Norwegian Sea. Millions of fish breed around the islands, and the world's largest deepwater **coral reef** lies offshore—as well as some of the deadliest **currents** on Earth.

Sperm whales and other whales visit the waters around the Lofoten Islands.

Aaron's rod is a **hardy** plant that grows on sea cliffs. Its flower petals are yellow, sometimes tipped with red.

Thousands of Atlantic puffins dive underwater to catch sand eels with their strong beaks. On the cliffs, the birds dig homes in which to nest.

29

Glossary

alpine Relating to high mountains

altitude The height of an object above sea level

aquatic Living in water

barren Having few or no plants

caldera A large volcanic crater, usually formed by a major eruption, after which the crater collapses

canopy The highest tree branches in a forest

coral reef A hard structure in the sea that is made from the remains of dead coral

crater A bowl-shaped hole around the opening of a volcano

current Water that is moving in one direction

delta The area where a river drops mud and sand as it enters a lake or ocean

dense Growing close together

dormant Inactive for now

eruptions Explosive blasts from volcanoes

foothills A hilly area at the base of a mountain range

glacier A large body of ice moving slowly down a valley

hardy Able to survive harsh conditions, such as extreme cold or heat

hibernate To take a very long, deep sleep, usually in winter

inlet A narrow sea channel that runs inland

invertebrate An animal that does not have a backbone

lagoon An area of salt water enclosed by a coral reef, sandbank, or rocks

limestone Rock formed from fossilized animal skeletons and shells

marine Living in the ocean

marsh An area of soft, wet land with many grasses and other plants

meltwater Water that results from glacier ice melting, usually in summer

migrated Traveled a long way for more plentiful food

native Living or growing naturally in an area

porous Having many small holes that soak up water

predators Animals that kill and eat other animals

prey Animals that are killed and eaten by other animals

rapids A section of river where the water flows very fast, often over rocks

reedbeds Large areas of tall, thin grasses called reeds

sheer Straight up and down

spawn To release or deposit eggs in a body of water

summit The very top

territory An area that an animal defends during the breeding season

tree line An imaginary line on a mountain that no trees can grow above

venom A chemical that some animals use to poison prey

venomous Producing chemicals that can injure or kill prey

vineyard Where grapes are grown, usually to make wine

Further Information

Books

Baxter, Roberta. *Learning about Europe*.
Lerner Publishing, 2015.

Knufinke, Joana Costa. *Europe*. Scholastic, 2019.

Miles, John. *Pathways Through Europe*.
Crabtree Publishing, 2019.

Rockett, Paul. *Mapping Europe*. Crabtree Publishing, 2017.

Websites

www.dkfindout.com/us/earth/continents/europe/
Find lots of interesting and fun facts about the
European continent here.

www.ducksters.com/geography/europe.php
This website has profiles of every country in Europe.

http://gowild.wwf.org.uk/regions/europe-fact-files
Discover more about your favorite animals in these
WWF fact files.

www.nationalgeographic.com/animals/index/
Type in the names of animals you're interested in and
get lots of fascinating facts about mammals, reptiles,
amphibians, fish, and birds.

Index